£8.95
£4.95

On Passage

On Passage

MIKE PEYTON

FERNHURST BOOKS

© Mike Peyton 1991

First published 1991 by
Fernhurst Books, 33 Grand Parade,
Brighton, East Sussex

ISBN 0 906754 66 6

Composition by CST, Hove
Printed by Hartnolls Ltd, Bodmin

Printed and bound in Great Britain

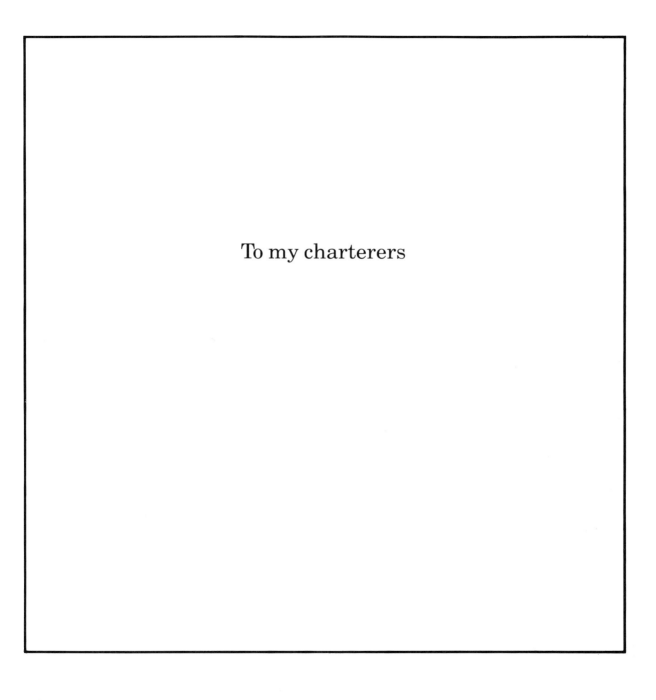

To my charterers

Acknowledgements
These cartoons are published with the kind permission of
Yachts & Yachting, Practical Boat Owner and *Yachting Monthly,*
where they first appeared.

Contents

— 1 —
ROUGH WATER

'Tell me again. How much is it we're saving on a bottle of gin?'

'Have you noticed that when you leave a boat on the
other side the weather improves, and when you go over
to sail it back it . . .'

'I told you we wouldn't be the only ones out.'

*'I don't give a damn if its confidence level is nine –
mine's zero.'*

'I can't understand why winter sailing isn't more popular.'

'Ready about!'

'I sometimes think the theory that sailing helps get rid
of stress is bull . . .'

'*Typical!*'

'Yes, it's good sailing – except we're running back to where we came from and not to where we're going.'

'*And in my experience, when a gale warning is wrong
the quickest way to put it right is to shake out the reefs.*'

'Stop fooling around and get on with it!'

— 2 —
JUST ADD WATER

'Why don't you take navigation classes?!!!'

'. . . and the boss said "Sometimes, Benson, I don't
think your mind's on your work".'

'I'll give you fifty to one his first words will be "Sorry, officer, I've a tide to catch".'

'That's fantastic. Do you want a crew?'

'We were thinking of getting something bigger.'

'Absolutely nothing to declare ossifer.'

'Hello again. Still on passage?'

PEYTON

'Watch him. He'll get you blotto, then persuade you to
let John crew him for the Channel Race . . .'

'We invariably recover them, Sir – admittedly with a
few cleats, sheaves and eyebolts added but, on the credit
side, varnished.'

'And another thing. Have you ever worked out how
much an hour it's costing to do this?'

'I got it cheap, last afternoon of the show.'

— 3 —
WATER PLEASE!

*'Now if this is CH2. The wind was sou'west, about a
five, and we were on starb . . .'*

'All season tuning it up for the Old Gaffers' Race and look what he does.'

'What do you mean, "Can I read it?" I don't need to.'

'And tell your mother why. I'd be club champion now
if you'd popped that spinnaker up when I told you.'

'Are you sure we have to leave it to starboard?'

'It's a split-pin. It's just hit me.'

'But he seemed so laid back when you introduced us at
the club . . .'

'Gone aground have they, and in our class. Jolly bad luck.'

'There's the mark. Leave it to port, then home, sixty miles to windward – alternatively there's the Restaurant de Ville two miles downwind.'

4
LOCAL WATER

'Starboard!'

'It doesn't seem such a good idea now!'

'Shall I hang on?'

'The last time I saw the boat keys was where you always leave them, on top of your desk and, may I add, "To be touched by no-one".'

'Not here! Wait until we're on board!'

'We're not here because it's romantic but because the holding is good and it's sheltered from the sixes and sevens forecast.'

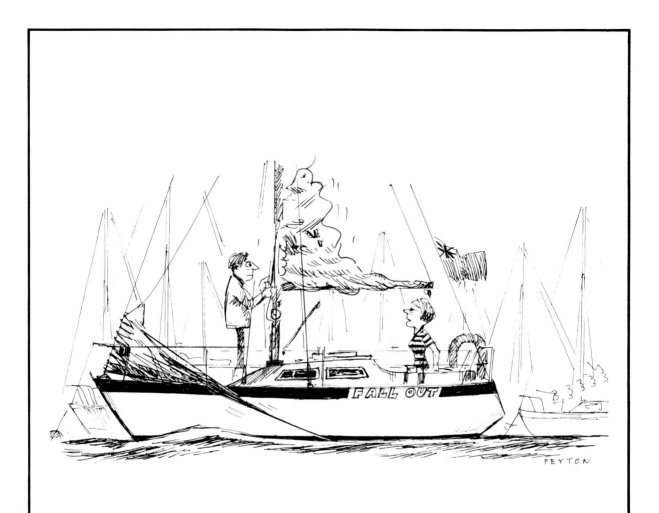

'I haven't touched the engine.'

— 5 —
WATER SHORTAGE

'Sorry to bother you, Mr Maynard. I know from your
secretary you're at a rather important meeting, but . . .'

'I imagine it's a mast and boom, but let's give them a few more minutes.'

'Doesn't that take you back, when you loved him so much
you chipped ballast, scrubbed bilges, anti-fouled . . .'

'What's a Point of Sale?'

'I don't want to spoil your day, Skip, but have you noticed these blisters?'

*'That's the drawback with navigation these days, too
damned accurate.'*

'It's 49½ minutes to low in Reeds, 48 minutes in the C.A. Handbook and 46¼ minutes in Macmillan's Silk Cut.'

'It's better than Howard's Way.'

'I don't want to be pessimistic but it's just gone low water.'

— 6 —
CONFINED WATER

*'It might seem a jolly spiffing sport to you, Carruthers,
but I don't think it will catch on.'*

'If it wasn't for this heater we'd be laid up and missing
all this fun.'

'Nothing against your cooking, Skip, but I'll wait until
we get in.'

'Relax, chaps. She was just travelling a bit faster than I thought.'

'Can you spare a minute, Skip?'

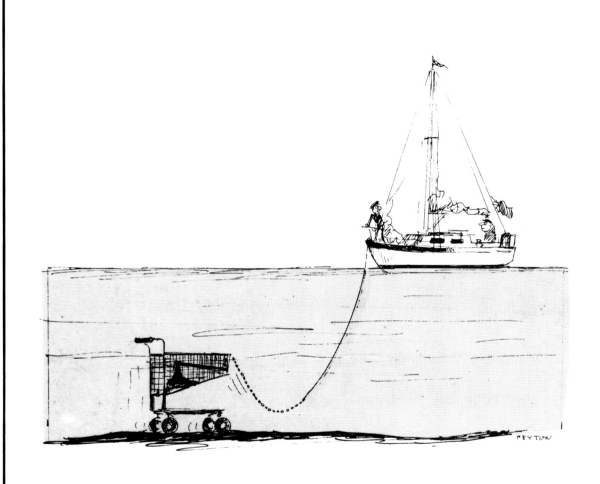

'We're dragging all right, and fast . . .'

'I'm sure you'll be able to buy him off.'

'We'll go alongside them. They look a friendly bunch.'

'What do you mean, "Reverse"?!!'

— 7 —
UNKNOWN WATER

'Non intende come ici.'

'It's a bit like those seamanship problems in yachting
mags, except we can't turn to page 147 for the answers.'

'That's exactly what they forecast.'

'What do you mean, "Beacon ahead." There's no beacon around here.'

'An unmarked wreck? It's about a billion to one chance.'

'That's the conical we were looking for all right.'

'Skip, you remember that gas rig that pinpointed our position . . .'

'Will we hit it? . . . A sixty-mile run across spring tides, three windshifts, John steering ten degrees off his entire watch, all that dodging about crossing the shipping lanes . . . You must be joking!'

'Is it still a spinnaker, Skip, or is it a staysail now?'

'Haven't you seen a waypoint before?'

'Have we passed? We were bang on.'

— 8 —
HOT WATER

'A toast – to the lady we all love.'

'In case you're curious it's a cake mixer — and I'll swap it for the GPS Navigator you've bought me.'

'*I fixed it temporarily.*'

'It's all right for you with a built-in crew. My blokes
listen to the shipping forecast and that's it.'

'Good Lord! Was it this weekend I invited you?'

'All I said was, "Here's a card for Aunty Freda", and he
said, "eff me, Anty Freeze", and he'd gone.'

'What are we?'

'I wouldn't mind if it was another woman, but a
sixty-year-old cutter that needs new garboards
and gaff-rigged at that!!'

'And no facetious remarks, "Lovely view you've got
Mrs Black." She's a bit touchy.'

'You mean to tell me that's the same price as a
spinnaker!'

'Well - at least we're insured'